Chicago WHITE SOX

KENNY ABDO

Fly!
An Imprint of Abdo Zoom
abdobooks.com

abdobooks.com

Published by Abdo Zoom, a division of ABDO, P.O. Box 398166, Minneapolis, Minnesota 55439.

Printed in the United States of America, North Mankato, Minnesota.
102025
012026

Photo Credits: AP Images, Getty Images, Shutterstock
Production Contributors: Kenny Abdo, Jennie Forsberg, Grace Hansen
Design Contributors: Candice Keimig, Neil Klinepier

Library of Congress Control Number: 2025936776

Publisher's Cataloging-in-Publication Data

Names: Abdo, Kenny, author.
Title: Chicago White Sox / by Kenny Abdo
Description: Minneapolis, Minnesota : Abdo Zoom, 2026 | Series: MLB teams | Includes online resources and index.
Identifiers: ISBN 9798384940142 (lib. bdg.) | ISBN 9798384940906 (ebook) | ISBN 9798384941286 (read-to-me ebook)
Subjects: LCSH: Chicago White Sox (Baseball team)--Juvenile literature. | Baseball teams--Juvenile literature. | Professional sports--Juvenile literature. | Sports franchises--Juvenile literature. | Major League Baseball (Organization)--Juvenile literature.
Classification: DDC 796.357--dc23

Table of CONTENTS

White Sox 4

Batter Up! 8

Grand Slams 14

Hall of Fame 24

Glossary 30

Online Resources 31

Index 32

WHITE SOX

With the Cubs taking care of the North Side of Chicago, Illinois, the White Sox have the South Side's bases covered!

MADRIGAL
1

With a history beginning in 1901, the South Siders have had their ups and downs but continue to prove they can still knock fans' socks off!

WORLD S
New Era Fits
Chicago
18
Chicago
24
KONERKO

BATTER UP!

The Chicago White Sox began play in the **American League** (**AL**) in 1901 as the White Stockings. That same year, the team made a buzz by winning the first AL **pennant**, exciting fans across Chicago!

The White Stockings changed its nickname to the White Sox in 1904. The team beat the favored Cubs to win its first World Series in 1906! Fans called their team the "Hitless Wonders" because they relied on strong pitching, not big hits.

FRANK ISBELL—2nd Baseman
White Sox, World's Champions

The White Sox won the World Series again in 1917. However, the good times would not last. In 1919, eight players were accused of taking a **bribe** to lose the World Series on purpose. Fans were upset and the White Sox name was ruined. The Black Sox Scandal, as it became known, left a dark cloud over the team for decades.

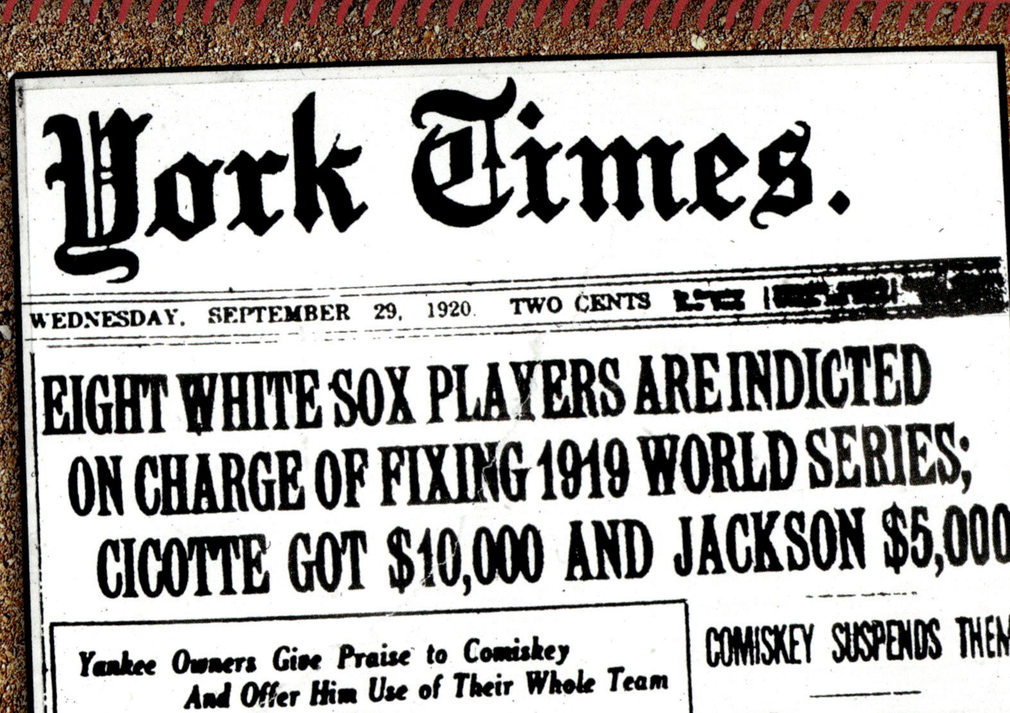

York Times.

WEDNESDAY, SEPTEMBER 29, 1920. TWO CENTS

EIGHT WHITE SOX PLAYERS ARE INDICTED ON CHARGE OF FIXING 1919 WORLD SERIES; CICOTTE GOT $10,000 AND JACKSON $5,000

Yankee Owners Give Praise to Comiskey And Offer Him Use of Their Whole Team

Following the announcement from Chicago yesterday that Owner Charles A. Comiskey had suspended two star pitchers, two regular infielders, his two leading outfielders and one utility player, Colonels Jacob Ruppert and T. L. Huston, owners of the New York Club, put

COMISKEY SUSPENDS THEM

Promises to Run Them Out of Baseball if

DIAMOND
PORTABLE ELECTRIC
THE STANDARD

GRAND SLAMS

The White Sox finally showed signs of hope in 2000. They won the **AL** Central and made the playoffs for the first time since 1993. Frank Thomas and Magglio Ordóñez led the way. That season, the Sox scored more runs than any other team.

icago
56

From 2001 to 2004, the White Sox saw some success with Mark Buehrle's strong pitching, which helped the team win 61 games. Paul Konerko hit 92 home runs and drove in 319 runs. In 2003, Frank Thomas hit his 400th career home run. Yet the championship **drought** continued.

Chicago
JENKS

In 2005, the White Sox ended their 88-year championship **drought**. The team made history by sweeping the Astros in four games to win the World Series! South Side fans finally got the victory they had waited for their entire lives.

The White Sox kept bringing the heat after their big 2005 win. In 2007, Buehrle threw a no-hitter, while Bobby Jenks tied an MLB **record** by **retiring** 41 batters in a row! In 2008, the team brought pride back to the South Side with 89 wins and another **AL** Central title.

NO-HITTER
4-18-07

The White Sox had a few short playoff runs but struggled to stay on top. In 2024, they set a **record** for the most losses in a MLB season and finished last in the **AL** Central. The team marked its 125th year in 2025. To celebrate, they improved their win total from 2024. Fans still hope the Sox can patch things up and start a new winning thread.

HALL OF FAME

Luis Aparicio thrilled fans as the speedy shortstop for the White Sox. He led the league in stolen bases every year from 1956 to 1962. In 1959, he stole 56 bases and won his second **Gold Glove Award**!

Aparicio also finished second in **AL** MVP voting while helping the White Sox win the **pennant** that year. He joined the Baseball Hall of Fame in 1984.

Frank Thomas crushed 448 home runs and drove in 1,465 runs with the White Sox. He won two MVP awards, played in five **All-Star** Games, and took home four Silver Slugger awards. Thomas hit over .300 in ten seasons and led the league in on-base percentage four times. He was named to the Hall of Fame in 2014.

Chicago

Harold Baines was a standout hitter for the White Sox for much of his 22-year career. He hit 221 home runs and collected 981 **RBIs** with the team, once holding several team **records**. Baines made six **All-Star** teams and won a Silver Slugger Award. He was named to the Baseball Hall of Fame in 2019.

GLOSSARY

All-Star – a yearly baseball contest where top players from the AL and the National League (NL) compete against each other, or the team made up of All-Star athletes.

American League (AL) – one of two 15-team leagues that make up MLB.

bribe – something promised or given to a person, such as money, as a way of getting that person to do a certain thing.

drought – a long period of time when a team does not win a major title or playoff series.

Gold Glove Award – an annual award given to the best fielders at each position in both the AL and NL.

pennant – the title achieved by the team that wins its division or league championship.

record – the total number of wins and losses a team has in a season; the achievement a player or team earns from doing something better than anyone before.

retire – to get a batter out.

Runs Batted In (RBI) – a statistic that credits a batter for making a play that allows a run to be scored.

ONLINE RESOURCES

To learn more about the Chicago White Sox, please visit abdobooklinks.com or scan this QR code. These links are routinely monitored and updated to provide the most current information available.

INDEX

Aparicio, Luis 24, 25

Astros (team) 19

Baines, Harold 29

Black Sox Scandal 12

Buehrle, Mark 17, 20

championships 10, 12, 19, 20

Cubs (team) 4, 10

Jenks, Bobby 20

Konerko, Paul 17

Ordóñez, Magglio 15

records 20, 22, 29

Thomas, Frank 15, 17, 26